Original title:
Ode to the Spider Plant

Copyright © 2025 Creative Arts Management OÜ
All rights reserved.

Author: Arabella Whitmore
ISBN HARDBACK: 978-1-80581-715-4
ISBN PAPERBACK: 978-1-80581-242-5
ISBN EBOOK: 978-1-80581-715-4

Homebound Navigator

In the corner, you stand tall,
A leafy ship with no sea at all.
With tendrils stretching every way,
You dance in sunlight, come what may.

Your leaves are like a map, they say,
Guiding me through my mundane day.
A navigator in this land of dust,
With you, dear friend, I always trust.

In the Embrace of Potted Dreams

In your pot, a world you hold,
Amongst the dirt, your dreams unfold.
Each leaf a tale of growth and cheer,
While I sip tea, you persevere.

You plot my path with every sprout,
While I just sit and start to pout.
Oh, what a life you seem to lead,
No want, no rush, just plant's own creed.

Verdant Elegy

I watched you sprout, a green delight,
With every inch, you reached new height.
But lo! A brown tip stole your glow,
What tragic fate you now bestow.

Yet in your flaw, we find some grace,
A quirky way to charm this space.
With winks of green, you make me laugh,
A little twist in nature's graph.

Guardian of Green Delights

Oh keeper of the cluttered room,
You flourish bright, despite the gloom.
With chubby leaves and roots so stout,
You guard my space, there's no doubt.

At times, you look quite wildly so,
A jungle vibe, you steal the show.
With every leaf, a smile you weave,
In your embrace, I truly believe.

The Leafy Lyricist

In corners danced the leafy folk,
With arms that sway, they twist and poke.
A giggle here, a chuckle there,
They charm the dust and tease the air.

Their leaves are pens, the soil their stage,
Each growing day, they turn a page.
Whispers of green, they come alive,
With every sprout, the fun will thrive.

A Garden's Gentle Heart

In pot and sun, a rebel stirs,
With little feet, it jigs and purrs.
A plant so bold with tiny spouts,
It giggles softly, shouts and shouts.

It plots to climb and stretch so high,
With leafy leaps that make you sigh.
A jumble of fun in every twist,
This darling green won't be dismissed.

The Cascading Jewel

Like a waterfall of emerald dreams,
It dances down with quirky schemes.
Hanging low, it waves hello,
In every drape, a show of glow.

With morning light, it sparkles bright,
A sight to see, what pure delight!
It sways and twirls with breezy flair,
A playful act beyond compare.

Skylines of Green

In rooftops' height, they light the skies,
A leafy crew with watchful eyes.
They peek and prance from every ledge,
A funny sight, they make a pledge.

To dance with clouds and laugh with birds,
In silent chats, they share their words.
With leafy friends, the skyline beams,
In laughter's breeze, they stitch their dreams.

Climbing to the Sun

In corners high, they start to creep,
With tiny tendrils, secrets to keep.
Reaching for light, in a comical race,
A green acrobat with a leafy face.

Each new leaf, a high five in green,
Waving around like a plant party scene.
In a pot they jive, like a dance on a whim,
Laughing at all who call them dim.

The Soft Whisperer of the Home

Whispers of green in the sunny nook,
A gentle giggle, like a funny book.
They sway and sway, with a cheeky cheer,
A softener of hearts, the actor here.

With leaves stretched out, they catch the light,
Sipping on sunshine, feeling just right.
They don't mind the dust, nor fuss to preen,
Just here for laughs, like a comic routine.

Leaves of Serenity

Serene they stand, with a wink and a nod,
Turning the mundane into a little odd.
Each green fringe giggles at life's busy race,
Offering calm with a leafy embrace.

They don't need much, just a bit of space,
And when you water, it's a splashy grace.
Every drop turned into a watery joke,
Creating green joy, like a playful poke.

Cascades of Vitality

Dripping green trails from their vibrant crowns,
Confetti of joy in these leafy towns.
Making the air dance with vitality,
They prance around, a green duality.

Like tiny ninjas on a jungle spree,
Chasing dust bunnies, as sprightly as can be.
In a riot of green, they shimmy and sway,
Bringing the laughter to every day.

Quiet Flourish in Our Space

A plant with curls that sprout and sway,
It dances lightly, come what may.
With leaves that stretch like lazy cats,
It makes the sun feel like a chat.

In corners where the shadows creep,
It smiles, inviting, not a peep.
A green confetti for the room,
A joyful splash that starts to bloom.

Resilience Wrapped in Green

Oh, fierce little fighter in a pot,
With roots that thrive and fight for a spot.
You share the light with every friend,
In life's wild jungle, you pretend.

Your leaves are tales of grit and cheer,
A tiny hero, bringing near.
You laugh at dust and drink the air,
In your green kingdom, we haven't a care.

The Lush Companion

With tendrils reaching, sweeping low,
You make our space a vibrant show.
In every twist, a laugh declared,
A leafy pal, it's quite the flair!

A friend who never talks too much,
But brightens days with every touch.
In the morning's sun, you just recline,
Chasing our worries, all in fine line.

Roots of Comfort

In a cozy pot where you reside,
Your leafy charm, our joyful guide.
They say that laughter's in the green,
But you, dear plant, reign like a queen.

With little babies trailing down,
You wear your crown without a frown.
In life's odd moments, you provide,
A twist of joy where we reside.

Guardians of the Urban Jungle

In a pot, they stand so proud,
Little stars in a leafy crowd.
With long arms that reach for air,
Pretending they just don't care.

Defenders of the dusty scene,
Waving leaves, they keep it green.
With every twist, a playful dance,
Inviting the curious glance.

A Journey of Green and Gold

On shelves, they spread their charm,
Dancing in the sunlight's warm.
Roots like fingers in the pot,
Grabbing snacks and things we got.

Each leaf whispers tales untold,
Secrets wrapped in green and gold.
With laughter in their lovely sway,
They turn our frowns to pure ballet.

The Hidden Touch of Nature

In cubicles, they take their stand,
A leafy friend, so bold and grand.
With faux leaves they cheer our plight,
Turning boring days to bright.

They catch our dust with every breath,
Giving life, and dodging death.
In every corner, they do thrive,
Invisible hugs, keeping us alive.

Tresses of Tranquil Harmony

With tresses long and leaves so sleek,
They stir up joy, we hear them speak.
A sprinkle of fun in plain view,
A comic twist in nature's hue.

Bouncing gently like a cheer,
They rescue us from urban fear.
A touch of green, a playful tease,
Bringing laughs with effortless ease.

Chasing Sunbeams with Leaves

In a pot by the window, you stretch and you yawn,
Reaching for sunlight, from dusk until dawn.
Your tips are a dance, like a wiggle and sway,
Those long, spindly arms shout, "Let's play all day!"

Little green dancer, what mischief you brew,
With each curious curl, you invite the zoo.
A cat in the corner, too jealous to wait,
Plots little escapes—he thinks you look great!

Financial planner of water and soil,
You sip from a cup, while I toil and toil.
With a whisper of laughter, I see your wise grin,
As you grow ever taller, inviting chagrin.

So here's to your antics, your thieving of sun,
Creating a jungle where chaos is fun.
You sly little sprout, always beckoning glee,
In your leafy embrace, forever I'll be!

A Tender Tale of Flora

In the corner, you wave with a cheeky delight,
Catching the whispers of soft morning light.
You gossip with dust bunnies, sharing the news,
Of all the adventures you choose to peruse.

Sprouting with flair, like a diva on stage,
Twisting and turning, you channel your rage.
For who needs a garden when one has a pot?
Your charm and your wit hit the humorous spot.

In a battle of wills with my cluttered old shelf,
You stand with such poise, like you're meant for yourself.

"Oh look," you proclaim, "I've toppled this mug,
Let's taste this adventure, it's surely a hug!"

With a sparkle and giggle, you brighten my days,
Proclaiming, "Let's live in the funniest ways!"
So here's to your splendor, you quirky green sprite,
In this tale of the flora, you shine oh so bright!

Spirals of Nature's Design

In pots they whirl with leafy grace,
Dancing lightly in their space.
With tendrils tangled, full of cheer,
They mimic hair when brushed with fear.

A spider plant, so bold and spry,
Catching dust bunnies as they fly.
With each green leaf, it's quite absurd,
Like a nature lover's friendly bird.

Embracing the Wandering Leaves

Oh, those leaves, they love to roam,
And take a trip around your home.
They sneak a peek at what you do,
Daring you to say, 'Who are you?'

In sunlight's rays, they work their mix,
A gossamer of leafy tricks.
Each step you take, they follow too,
As if to say, 'We're here with you!'

Nature's Velvet Charm

With textures soft upon the skin,
These plants invite you to jump in.
They sway and giggle in the breeze,
Demanding love with leafy tease.

Each new leaf, a cheeky grin,
An emerald smile; oh, let's begin!
In potted houses, drama thrives,
Who knew such charm could come from lives?

Poetry Woven in Green

In corners bright, their feels unite,
A tapestry of green delight.
They plot and scheme with chlorophyll,
A leafy joke, a topsy thrill.

In sunlight's gaze, they wink and tease,
Whispering secrets in the breeze.
They throw a party, leafy cheer,
Inviting us all to join right here.

Mosaic of Lushness

In a pot, you reign with glee,
Your leaves dance, wild and free.
With green fingers you conspire,
A quirky plant, we admire!

Your babies dangle, what a show,
Like tiny troops, they come and grow.
Repotted with a confident cheer,
A leafy squad, no end is near!

Sunlight bathes your leafy crown,
You wave at neighbors, never frown.
Chasing dust bunnies round the room,
A fun sensation, free from gloom!

Each leaf is a story, don't you see?
You're a jester in green history.
With laughter sprouting from each stem,
A mosaic of joy is what you hem!

Kindred Spirits of Foliage

Oh, how you skitter on the ledge,
With your long green tendrils, you pledge.
To keep the air fresh and breezy,
In your presence, we all feel easy!

In every twist, a secret lies,
Your playful nature, oh what a surprise!
Raising eyebrows with your leafy charms,
You call for hugs, not just alarms!

You chat with the cat, who's quite bemused,
In this jungle, none are bruised.
Together you plot atop the shelf,
Like two green souls, just being yourself!

A partnership of laughter and light,
In pots and soils, you dance at night.
Oh leafy friend, you're quite a hit,
In this green world, we all commit!

Breathing Life into Spaces

In my corner, you stand with flair,
Breathing life without a care.
You sip sunlight, your favorite drink,
A jolly plant, what do you think?

Dust gathers on the window sill,
You shake it off, with style and thrill.
No static here, just a happy vibe,
You make this house alive, no jibe!

Your leaves are like whispers in the air,
Spreading joy everywhere.
Bring on the laughter, the jokes you weave,
A pot of giggles, hard to believe!

Oh, the tales you'd tell if you could,
Of every nook, of every wood.
Happily living, a comedy play,
In this lush home, we dance and sway!

Folly of the Four-Legged & Leafed

Four-legged friends, they prance and pose,
While you chillax in leafy clothes.
They sniff and bounce, eyeing your grace,
But your composure wins the race!

With paws and claws, they seem to jest,
A foliage showdown, a tricky test.
Yet you sway, a master of charm,
With every leaf, you sound the alarm!

You're the ruler of this humble space,
While they dash around, you hold your place.
A still ambassador of peace and green,
Who knew life with pets could be such a scene?

So here's to the laughter we share each day,
In this leafy chaos, we find our way.
Together we bloom, a comedic blend,
With four legs and leaves, the joy won't end!

The Green Guardian's Embrace

In the corner, sprightly green,
A cheerful smile, it's rarely seen.
With leaves like fingers dancing free,
It beckons me, come look and see!

A pot of joy, it sways in glee,
Chatting with dust balls, oh so carefree.
It's the guardian of all my mess,
With roots that gossip, I must confess!

When friends arrive, it takes the stage,
Trimming all doubts; it's quite the sage.
In its spiky hair, I see such flair,
A leafy crown, a royal affair!

With water drops, it plays and sings,
My trusty friend, with many things.
Each leaf a story, each sprout a tale,
A green sensation that will prevail!

Symphony of the Airborne Roots

In sunlight bright, the leaves do sway,
With laughter loud, they greet the day.
A concert hall of verdant cheer,
The whispers of nature, oh so near!

With kindred spirits in terracotta,
They hum a tune like sweet piñata.
A chorus formed from roots that dance,
Inviting all for a leafy prance!

Tiny pups hang like curious notes,
On the breeze, they sail like boats.
A jolly crowd of green delight,
Making every room feel just right!

Their laughter echoes, wise and bold,
In a language of green, they unfold.
A symphony that fills the air,
With spider plants, I've found my share!

Nature's Wandering Performer

A dazzling act upon the sill,
This performer has such a thrill.
With dangling tendrils in the light,
It dances daily, what a sight!

The curtain rises, showtime's here,
With a tilt and sway, it draws a cheer.
It leaps around, a sprightly sprite,
In every corner, pure delight!

With every sip, it feasts and grows,
On clumsy moments, how it glows!
Each leaf a bow, each sprout a grin,
In its verdant world, fun begins!

It juggles sunlight, just like a pro,
Turning my room into a show.
With capers grand, it steals the scene,
The greenest star I've ever seen!

A Tapestry of Verdant Life

In tangled threads of vibrant hue,
A tapestry woven, all askew.
Each leaf a stitch, so deftly spun,
Together they shine, oh what fun!

With quirky curls and playful bends,
They weave their magic, loose ends friends.
In pots and nooks, they spread delight,
A lively artwork, pure and bright!

They laugh at tasks left undone,
A vibrant crew that's never run.
With cozy vibes, they rule the day,
In their green kingdom, we come to play!

Oh, join the dance, embrace the mess,
In this living quilt, I must confess.
With every twist, I find my cheer,
A verdant life that's always near!

A Touch of Nature's Palette

In pots of green, they shimmy and sway,
With leaves like ribbons, brightening the day.
They hang with flair, a green confetti,
Whispering secrets, so cute and petty.

A sip of water? Oh, what a show!
They drink it up like a thirsty pro.
In sunlight's glow, they seem to cheer,
A leafy party, come join us here!

Their roots stretch down, a hidden dance,
In soil they twirl, given half a chance.
Yet watch your step, they might just tease,
With playful drapes that flutter in the breeze.

In corners bright, they petal out style,
Winking at you with a cheeky smile.
Nature's prankster in every green plume,
Making your space feel like a bloom room.

Ribbons of Soft Resilience

Little green wonders in the morning light,
They droop and they dangle, quite a sight!
Like nature's jester with a playful wink,
They spread their joy, don't even think.

Each leaf's a ribbon, fluttering free,
They giggle in sunshine, just wait and see.
When dust creeps in, they raise a fuss,
"Bring on the spritz!" they shout in trust!

A spider web's envy, they dangle and peep,
In a cheerful chorus, they leap and they leap.
With little green babies popping out in glee,
It's a party of leaves, and you're the VIP!

A dance of greens, oh, what a tease,
With every sprout, they aim to please.
In a world of dull, they stand so bright,
A soft resilience, a pure delight!

The Green Ballet

On the windowsill, they take their stance,
Swaying gently, as if in a dance.
With leaves that pirouette in the air,
An emerald ballet, beyond compare.

Each tendril sways in a fluttering tune,
Like tiny dancers beneath the moon.
Their steps are simple, but full of grace,
Creating a stage in every little space.

They twirl and twist, the sunlight they crave,
In nature's theatre, it's they who wave.
Watch them lean in to take a bow,
Each leaf a star in the here and now.

So here's to the plants in a green ballet,
With their leafy moves, they brighten the day.
In this joyful scene, you'll surely find
A giggle or two, if you're of good mind!

Leafy Meditations

In corners calm, they sit and plot,
With leafy thoughts that aren't forgot.
Wiggly tendrils pondering the light,
A meditative dance, serene delight.

They catch the sun like a little spy,
Curled up in silence, oh so spry.
With wisdom of green, they quietly teach,
How to sway gently, without a breach.

In stillness found, they laugh at the fuss,
"Relax," they seem to say, "What's the rush?"
With a humorous twist and a leafy grin,
In their peaceful presence, you'll find the win.

So raise a glass to the plants that play,
In playful tones, they brighten the way.
With leafy meditations, both wise and sweet,
They'll tickle your heart with their rhythmic beat.

Nature's Suspended Symphony

In pots so grand, a show so bright,
A green ensemble, a charming sight.
With tendrils dangling, a playful tease,
They sway and dance with the slightest breeze.

They catch the dust, they catch the light,
In sunny spots, they hold on tight.
With leaves like ribbons, they flutter so free,
Nature's jesters, in glee we see.

A curious critter thinks they're a snack,
But oh dear friend, you've lost your track.
They're not just plants, they're pals in bloom,
In viney chaos, they fill the room.

So here's to the greens, the joys they bring,
A wonderful show, nature's jesting fling.
With each little leaf, they tickle our hearts,
In the leafy lounge, every humor starts.

The Leafy Labyrinth

In corners high, a jungle grows,
With spiraled greens, a plant encore.
They twist and turn like a merry maze,
A leafy labyrinth, in sunlight's gaze.

On adventurous days, I play hide and seek,
Amongst these leaves, it's fun, not bleak.
Where did the cat hide, where's my shoe?
In this green tangle, who knows what's true?

They wave and whisper, secrets to share,
With every leaf, there's fun in the air.
A game of tag with dust bunnies too,
In this jungle home, chaos ensues.

So here we laugh in this verdant space,
In the leafy labyrinth, life's a race.
With every twist, there's joy in sight,
In nature's charm, we find delight.

A Dance Amongst Shadows

In dim-lit rooms, they sway and play,
With shadows dancing at end of day.
They stretch their limbs, a quirky sight,
A leafy ballet, pure delight.

With every flicker from candle's flame,
Their graceful forms know no shame.
As they prance around, the cat jumps high,
Oh dear, what a show, oh my, oh my!

They flirt with curtains, they tease the air,
Spinning tales of laughter — who would dare?
A thespian cast in a leafy play,
In a dance with the shadows, night turns to day.

So let's all join in this leafy cheer,
Where shadows mingle, far and near.
In the twilight glow of our leafy space,
We laugh and dance at our merry pace.

The Breath of the Living Room

In cozy nooks, they hold their sway,
A fresh embrace at close of day.
With every leaf, a breath is found,
In this living room, joy does abound.

They stretch towards windows, seeking light,
While I sip tea, a cozy sight.
As I ponder life, they nod and sway,
"Join the green team, come what may!"

They whisper secrets to the fold,
Sharing stories, both new and old.
With every quirk, they steal the show,
In this room of laughter, they help us grow.

So here's to the greens, the air they share,
In every corner, their charm is rare.
In the breath of our living room bright,
A symphony of joy, in leafy delight.

Dance of the Chlorophyll Spirits

In the pot where green fingers sway,
Dancing leaves laugh through the day.
Their playful jig brings joy anew,
Watch them twirl in the living room view.

Spin and sway, little plants so spry,
Twirling in sunlight, reaching for the sky.
With each bounce, they tease my cat,
Chasing shadows, what a silly spat!

They whisper secrets in rustling air,
Making my worries vanish with flair.
Green little spirits with legs so spry,
In this green world, let out a sigh!

Each leaf a dancer, a jittery sprite,
Frolicking freely, a comical sight.
Join the fun, oh silly friend,
In the dance of leaves, let laughter blend.

The Leafy Lullaby

Softly now, the leaves do croon,
Swaying gently, like a cartoon.
Hush your worries, let them go,
In leafy arms, relaxation flows.

Little green gigglers, sing their tune,
A lullaby beneath the moon.
They hum sweet beats, playful and spry,
Resting together, you and I.

Petals chuckle as breezes roam,
In this little green leafy home.
With every sigh, they share a glance,
Inviting us all to join their dance.

So close your eyes, enjoy the night,
On leafy beds, it feels just right.
In their embrace, soft dreams take flight,
A leafy lullaby, pure delight!

Guardian of the Indoor Oasis

In the corner, a watchful eye,
A green protector, oh my, oh my!
With every leaf, it guards the space,
An indoor fortress, a leafy embrace.

Immovable yet full of charm,
With arms that spread, no need for alarm.
Its playful stance invites the muse,
While teasing cats with leafy ruse!

A sentinel of the indoor plot,
Hiding treasures within its lot.
What secrets lie in its green expanse?
Adventure awaits, if you dare take a chance.

So raise your glass to this leafy sage,
The guardian here for every age.
In laughter and joy, it leads the way,
To a whimsical world where we all play.

Threads of Life in Sunlit Corners

In corners bright, green threads are spun,
Life awakens, oh what fun!
Each leaf a whisper, a story untold,
In beams of sunlight, they glimmer like gold.

Winding vines with a cheeky twist,
A tapestry formed, you can't resist.
Life's little wonders, in foliage wrapped,
With giggles and grins, softly entrapped.

Tickling the air, they plot and scheme,
A forest of dreams, or so it seems.
Each dangling leaf a tale to share,
Of silly moments, floating in air.

So let's celebrate each leafy dance,
In sunlit corners, take a chance.
With threads of life, let laughter rise,
In the joyful web where green spirit lies.

Colors of Connection

In a pot, a spider plant sits,
With leaves like ribbons, tiny bits.
It wiggles and jiggles in the light,
A dancer at dawn, oh what a sight!

Roots like spaghetti, tangled and cute,
A family reunion, oh what a hoot!
Its babies dangle like a weird charm,
Who needs a dog when you've got this farm?

Green fingers waving, such a delight,
Regaling tales of last night's flight.
In the jungle of my living room space,
A spider muse with a leafy face!

Perched on the shelf, it's a real showstopper,
Wraps itself around like an optimistic flopper.
It's not just a plant, it's my little sidekick,
In the garden of life, it's the best kind of trick!

Storylines in the Green Canopy

In the corner, a leafy explorer,
Plotting stories that grow ever more.
Each sprout a chapter, each leaf a tale,
Of garden adventures, both epic and frail.

Hanging out, it waves to the sun,
Sipping on light, oh what fun!
A green diva with roots so deep,
Whispering secrets that make me leap.

A spider in waiting, pretend it's a friend,
Rehearsing its lines as the daylight bends.
In the pot it spins yarns, daring and bright,
As I chuckle at its comical plight.

With tiny babies, it starts a parade,
Each one a diplomat, unafraid.
The bravest of plants, no fear of heights,
Throwing green parties on whimsical nights!

The Sway of Life

In my house, it sways with flair,
A leafy motion, light as air.
Like a dance partner, oh so spry,
Twirling gently as we walk by.

It whispers jokes in the morning sun,
Lifting spirits, having fun.
With every breeze, a little jig,
Who knew plants could dance so big?

A wiggle here, a shake there,
A green confetti, vibrant and rare.
Life's not dull with this tagalong,
In the comfort of home, it's where we belong!

Catching dust bunnies, playing hide and seek,
Offering laughs when the days grow bleak.
With every sway, joy starts to spread,
A plant full of life, dancing instead!

Messages in the Foliage

Amidst the green, thoughts come alive,
Messages hidden, watch them thrive.
Each leaf a letter, tangled in fun,
Whispers of joy, blessings spun.

With each new sprout, a secret unfolds,
Tales of adventures, brave and bold.
They giggle at jokes that only they know,
In the greenery, good vibes flow.

Swinging and swaying, oh what a sight,
Preaching cheer from morning till night.
A therapist in pot, so wise yet spry,
With every green nod, a wink to the sky.

From my windowsill, it sends out glee,
Inviting the world to come and see.
Its greenery glimmers, a joyful spree,
Planting smiles like seeds, just let it be!

Reflections in Green

In the corner, bright and spry,
A leafy friend who waves goodbye.
She catches dust and dreams in strands,
A jungle queen with sprawling hands.

When watering's done, she looks so proud,
Bowing gently, a leafy crowd.
Each new shoot is a playful tease,
Making me laugh with utter ease.

Her babies dangle, looking down,
Tiny clowns in a green gown.
They whisper secrets, "We're just fine!"
In this home, they truly shine.

With every glance, she plays her part,
The king of plants, the queen of heart.
In her embrace, I find my cheer,
An eco-joker, ever near.

The Secret Language of Leaves

In whispers soft, the leaves conspire,
Sharing tales of sun and fire.
A tiny nod, a gentle sway,
In leafy lingo, they play all day.

They gossip 'bout the dust bunnies here,
Wit so sharp, it brings a cheer.
Chasing shadows on the wall,
With every tilt, they have a ball.

"Watch us dance!" they seem to shout,
In their pot, they twist about.
A flamboyant troupe in leafy stage,
Comedic timing from a sage.

When watering time comes round,
They perk up high, simply unbound.
With every droplet, they break into song,
In their green world, I feel I belong.

An Offering of Verdancy

Oh plant of green, so full of cheer,
You make my windowsill appear.
With leaves that dangle, sway, and zoom,
You've turned my home to a jungle room.

Who needs a pet when leafy friends,
Can mimic chats and make amends?
They roll their leaves in playful jest,
So laid-back, they always rest.

Each new shoot is a party guest,
A wobbly friend that's never stressed.
They sprout and stretch with every glance,
Inviting me to join the dance.

A comic troupe in pots so small,
With every leaf, they enthrall.
Offering smiles, a little glee,
My verdant pals, wild and free.

The Comfort of Vita

In life's chaos, there you stand,
A leafy blessing, a gentle hand.
With every curl and twist, you cheer,
Bringing joy to those who near.

Oh, how you thrive with just some light,
A champion plant, a true delight.
You don't ask much, just love and care,
In your embrace, worries are rare.

You sway and bounce with every breeze,
Creating comfort that aims to please.
A soft reminder in this strife,
That humor's found in leafy life.

Just a glance at your green hue,
Makes my stress drift, like morning dew.
With you around, I can't complain,
A little giggle in your green domain.

Vibrations from the Verdant World

In a pot with flair so bright,
The plant dances in morning light.
It's green, it's sprightly, full of glee,
A jungle gym for a busy bee.

With leaves that stretch in a playful pose,
It wiggles like it really knows.
I swear it's groovin' to tunes unheard,
While I sip tea, feeling absurd.

Tiny shoots hang down like hair,
Whispering secrets, what a pair!
Is it a plant or my best friend?
I guess the support will never end!

In this green corner, we chuckle and share,
Mysteries of plant life, with utmost care.
With water and laughter, we're growing tall,
Who knew plant life could be such a ball?

Echoes of the Silver Leaves

Reflecting on the colors bright,
A little spy in the garden's sight.
With silver leaves that catch the breeze,
It seems to giggle with perfect ease.

Oh, how it sways with silly style,
Each leaf a dancer, each leaf a smile.
I watch it wiggle, think it's wise,
Actually plotting a prize in disguise.

Tendrils whisper of secrets sly,
"Water me, please, or I may cry!"
It pouts when dry, all droopy and bent,
But comes alive when the sun is sent!

This pot-bound buddy lifts my gloom,
Green therapy in a sunny room.
With tipsy poses, it steals the show,
In echoes of laughter, we together grow.

Shadows of the Sultry Sun

Under the sun, its leaves take flight,
Doing the cha-cha with pure delight.
In the soft glow of day's warm rays,
It struts its stuff in playful ways.

A loopy plant with a sense of fun,
Checks its reflection, "Ain't I the one?"
With shadows dancing upon the floor,
It knows how to party, and then some more!

Watching it grow is quite the thrill,
Whispers and giggles make time stand still.
With a twist here, a turn there,
I swear it's putting on quite the fair!

Beneath the sun's gaze, we share a laugh,
A green companion on my leafy path.
In this sultry heat, let's just declare,
Life's better with a plant that knows how to care.

The Web of Life within Four Walls

In this cozy nook, a spider plant hangs,
Casting green shadows, singing sweet twangs.
In its leafy embrace, I find my way,
Wishing for a friend in the fray of the day.

Creeping and crawling, it threads through my heart,
A jester in green, playing its part.
With tendrils dangling, it sways with glee,
Reminding me gently, "Hey, just be free!"

It whispers softly, "No need to rush,"
As time takes its turn, offering a hush.
With laughter and love in this little space,
The web of life weaves a warm embrace.

So here's to the plant, my leafy muse,
In this four-walled world, we happily cruise.
With each little laugh, a bond we create,
In the web of life, we both celebrate!

Sustaining the Urban Soul

In pots they perch, green ninja spies,
With leaves like stars, they seek the skies.
They drink up water, but spill none at all,
In their leafy kingdom, they stand so tall.

We chat with them, our leafy pals,
They nod their heads, giving us gales.
With roots like webbed feet, they take a stroll,
In the urban jungle, they play their role.

A dance of photosynthesis, what a sight,
Turning sunlight into their delight.
They whisper secrets of the city's heart,
Creating laughter that never departs.

So here's to plants that grow and thrive,
In every pot, they keep us alive.
With humor and charm, they keep it light,
Thank you, dear greens, for the endless delight!

Ephemeral Beauty in a Clay Pot

In my kitchen sits a pot that sings,
With little green leaves that flop and swing.
Each twist and turn, a daring ballet,
Taking the crown for the best display.

They've got the flair, they've got the charm,
Just a bit of water can do no harm.
When friends come over, they steal the show,
Cracking jokes with every new grow.

These humble heroes of household bliss,
With playful antics, you won't want to miss.
They laugh at dust and hoot at gloom,
Reviving spirits in every room.

Oh plant of joy, so bright, so spry,
With you around, it's hard to sigh.
In clay it sits, a treasure so rare,
A green comedian with flair to spare!

Cradle of Growth and Harmony

In corners dark, the green ones dwell,
Filling the room with a nature spell.
With their long green tails, they wave and sway,
Creating a peace that's here to stay.

When I forget to water, they just grin,
With roots so strong, they wear the win.
They laugh at neglect, they chuckle with ease,
In this happy home, they spread the tease.

Their leaves a canvas for stories untold,
In sunlit patches, their laughter unfolds.
They hug the pots, as snug as a bug,
In this quirky scene, it's all a shrug.

Here's to the green, that brings us cheer,
In quirky pots, they persevere.
With each little sprout, they take a stand,
A circus of greens in a waiting hand!

A Living Elegy

In leafy towers, they reach for dreams,
With roots that wriggle and sprout wild schemes.
They dance to the tune of a watering can,
With every droplet, part of their plan.

Sipping sunlight with a cheeky grin,
They know the secrets that lie within.
With every new leaf, a giggle well earned,
In the sitcom of life, their wisdom's discerned.

Creating shadows, they conspire with light,
In a playful duel, they're a true sight.
With a bounce in their leaves, they tell their tales,
Of urban jungles and wind-whipped gales.

So join in the fun, let plants take the lead,
In the silly world where greens are freed.
They may be humble, but in their own way,
They reign supreme, come shout hooray!

Vines in the Light

In the window, there she grows,
With leaves that twist, and leaves that pose.
She waves her arms with such delight,
A green ballet in sunny light.

When friends come over, they all yell,
"What's that lively lady? She's quite swell!"
I shrug and smile, say it's my jam,
Proudly showcasing her leafy glam.

Sometimes she sneezes, drops a leaf,
Causing me moments of sheer disbelief.
"Don't worry, love, you'll grow anew,"
I assure her, "with plenty to do!"

With every twist, she conquers space,
In every corner, she leaves her trace.
A green performer, never shy,
I think she winks as days go by.

Confidence in Green

Striking a pose in shades so bold,
She's got the moves, or so I'm told.
No one can match her leafy grace,
In this plant game, she sets the pace.

When she leans left, it's a plant boogie,
Got her style sharp, never foggy.
With every twist and sprout, she shows,
Confidence grows, that much I know!

Sometimes she blushes, it's hard to miss,
When I bring home that garden bliss.
But she struts right back, holds her head high,
"Watch out, world, I'm here to fly!"

So raise your glass to the green queen,
Living her life like a vibrant dream.
In our home, she's the star of the show,
With roots that dig deep, she's ready to grow!

Serenity in Home

In a cozy corner, she finds her place,
A leafy lady with a gentle grace.
While I sip tea and sink in my chair,
She nods along without a care.

Whispers of green in a room so still,
Even calm moments can give a thrill.
Her leaves dance softly in the breeze,
Making my heart hum with such ease.

As she dangles down, it feels like magic,
A leafy spell that's far from tragic.
"Is it me or the plant?" I'd surely muse,
When peace rolls in like morning's muse.

At night, she glimmers, a sight to adore,
In shadows softly she starts to implore.
"Stay close, dear friend, let worries subside,"
In her company, I take it in stride.

Lattice of the Living

A lattice formed of greens galore,
With tendrils reaching, wanting more.
She climbs up high, seeks out the sun,
In her leafy world, she's having fun.

Lines and patterns like a fine art,
In every twist, she plays her part.
Neighbors peek over with envious eyes,
"What's that plant? It's quite a surprise!"

"Just a little charm!" I proudly declare,
"She knows how to live without a care."
She leaves a trail of giggles and glee,
As if she knows she's a sight to see.

In this lattice of joy, she weaves her tale,
With each new sprout, she sets her sail.
Let's share a laugh with our green, leafy friend,
In this living tapestry, the fun won't end!

Heartbeats in Chlorophyll

With every tick, she breathes and glows,
Life in green, how well she knows.
A friend who laughs in shades of bright,
Bringing joy from morning to night.

She sways to tunes of a silent beat,
Leaves rustling softly, her rhythm sweet.
"Hey there," I say, "you're quite the sprite!"
With chlorophyll dreams, she takes to flight.

In every corner, she spreads her cheer,
A heartbeat echoing, soft and clear.
Together we dance, through laughter and glee,
In sync with the pulse of nature's decree.

So here's to you, my planty delight,
With roots in the ground and joy in flight.
May our heartbeats sync in perfect play,
Living our lives in a green ballet!

Whispers of Everyday Eden

In the corner sits a leafy cheer,
Stretching limbs with a sly little sneer.
Potted dreams dance in the sun,
Watching us scurry, oh what fun!

Cats can't resist, oh what a scene,
Tangled in green, living the dream.
A spider plant's charm, so laid back,
It holds the fort, no fear of attack.

Water me, don't drown me says the leaf,
In this garden chaos, I find relief.
Taking care feels like a fine prank,
Oh, to be green, with no need to thank!

As I dust off my worries each day,
Funny little green friend keeps gloom at bay.
In every corner, its laughter swings,
Oh, the joy that a plant like this brings!

Cascading Memories in Greenery

Tiny green warriors, they leap and twist,
In their jungle kingdom, none can resist.
A fountain of joy in a humble pot,
With their spaghetti strands, they hit the spot.

Mischief lurks in their droopy charms,
Wrapping around objects, causing alarms.
One wrong move and they're on the floor,
A tangle of laughter and just a bit more!

Every leaf a story, every pull a laugh,
With these green soldiers, I'm on my path.
They cheerfully whisper 'don't take life too tight',
Grow wild, my friend, and relish your plight!

Nature's comedians, oh what a team,
Sprouting joy and the occasional scream.
In the light of the sun, they fuzzily cheer,
Cascading memories we wish to hold dear!

Homegrown Soliloquy

In my home, greenery hosts a play,
Leafy actors dance in a glorious display.
With every new shoot, there's laughter to share,
Whispering secrets without a care.

Leaning over, saying, 'I'm feeling quite fab!',
Inoculating the air with their leafy jab.
Critique my attempts, oh I'm such a novice,
But these resilient greens are my happy office.

Each little baby, a sprout of delight,
Entwined conversations last through the night.
A room full of jokes with a botanical twist,
'One more watering?' —they laugh and insist.

Homegrown companions, in sun and in shade,
With curly green fingers, life's worries cascade.
In this leafy sanctuary, laughter prevails,
Jointly, we flourish, with joyous tales!

Revelry of the Resilient Ribbons

Ribbons of green, oh what a sight!
Swinging and swirling, with pure delight.
Dress me up, tie me down, oh what fun,
With plant-party vibes, we've only begun!

Tugging the strands, they tickle my nose,
These leafy pranksters, in bright repose.
'Not too much water!' they all seem to cry,
While I giggle and watch them sway high and dry.

Catching the flats, they're masters of style,
In their green shenanigans, I wear a smile.
Joking together in our cozy nook,
As they whisper secrets, which I can't overlook.

The revelry blooms, with laughter profound,
In their woven embrace, love knows no bound.
Echoes of green from the corners, they spread,
Where playful ribbons frolic, life's painted red!

Dance of the Leafy Ribbons

In the corner, a green ballerina sways,
With fronds that twist in a graceful haze.
Each leaf a pirouette, a leafy delight,
In the sunlight, she dances, oh what a sight!

Pot-bound but spry, with a wink and a twirl,
She juggles her pot, oh what a girl.
Twirling in circles, she plots her escape,
From shelf confinement, she dreams of great shapes.

Dust bunnies cheer, as she spins along,
The houseplants all hum a supportive song.
With potted pals, they form a tight crew,
Bouncin' in rhythm, with leaves shiny and new!

So raise your glasses, let's have a toast,
To the leafy ribbons we love the most.
In this green ballet, let laughter abound,
For in plant dance-offs, joy can be found!

Spirit of the Nurtured Fern

In a pot, she thrives, the fern of delight,
With feathery fronds, oh, what a sight!
She waves at the passersby with a giggle,
Her tendrils all swaying, it's hard not to wiggle!

Her leaves play peekaboo under sun's rays,
Like introverts thriving in their own ways.
When she catches a breeze, it tickles her glee,
And she leans to the side, sharing her spree!

With a sprinkle of water, she puffs up with pride,
Singing in silence, her joy she won't hide.
In the jungle of pots where her buddies reside,
She's the queen of the ferns, all leafy and spry!

So let's celebrate her, in laughter and cheer,
For this nurtured spirit brings joy all year.
With every soft curl, she brings smiles galore,
In the kingdom of greens, she's the one we adore!

Lullaby of the Leafy Lace

Hush now, dear plant, as night draws near,
Your leafy lace drapes, so delicate, dear.
With nighttime whispers, the shadows play,
Your elegance shimmers, in a dreamy ballet.

Your leaves are like ribbons, a soft gentle light,
Dancing through darkness, enchanting the night.
With each gentle wave, a soft giggle flows,
Spinning the tales that only you know.

From window to ceiling, you gracefully climb,
Telling tall stories, with whimsy and rhyme.
Your laughter is subtle, like raindrops that fall,
With a whisper to dreams, you enchant us all!

So settle, dear beauty, let the moonlight embrace,
And revel in quiet, your sleepy-laced grace.
For in every fold, there's a whole world to see,
A lullaby woven in leafy jubilee!

Tangled in Tranquility

In a wild tangle, there lies a charm,
With creaky old leaves that mean no harm.
Each twist and turn, a story unwinds,
In this cozy corner, tranquility finds.

Oh, the chaos of greens, what a glorious sight,
Like a frenzied dance party in soft moonlight!
Where spiderlings giggle, and pot friends collide,
In this leafy escapade, we all want to ride.

When the cat jumps by, there's a playful scare,
But our leafy companions – they don't seem to care.
They rustle and shake, "Just chill out, my friend,
We're tangled in peace, we're here to transcend!"

So let's toast to this chaos, so vibrant and free,
Where each laugh and leaf tells a story of glee.
In the charming disaster, fun moments abound,
Tangled in tranquility, our joy can be found!

Secrets in the Soil's Embrace

In a pot, with roots so sly,
A leafy trickster waves goodbye.
Spreading joy with every sprout,
Bouncing back, without a doubt.

Whispers of soil, tales untold,
They giggle and dance, bold and bold.
Green fingers peek from plastic nights,
Spreading laughter in sunny sights.

When a neighbor's cat strolls by,
Plant's a jester, oh my, oh my!
A tap dance of leaves, what a show,
Though they don't care, it's all for show.

Beneath the dirt, secrets hum,
"Water me less, just a crumb!"
With every sip, they stretch and glide,
The world's best comedian, they confide.

The Resilient Trailblazer

In the corner with a grin so wide,
A green explorer, full of pride.
Stretching limbs, up to the sun,
Who knew a plant could have such fun?

Defying rules, they reach and sway,
Not a care come what may.
Chasing light, they stumble and flop,
But never fear, they won't stop!

With a roguish curl and a playful twist,
In indoor jungles, they can't be missed.
Waving at dust, like an old friend,
"Water me more, it's all pretend!"

They know no bounds, no fears to face,
Just a dash of green, pure grace.
In the game of life, they play to win,
Laughing at troubles with a leafy grin!

Threads of Resilience

In a pot, a tangle of cheer,
Threads of green, oh what a sphere!
They twist and turn, a playful waltz,
Not taking life too seriously, at all!

With spider-like moves, they shimmy and sway,
Breaking record for the laziest day.
Roots in the dirt, partying hard,
Shouting to the sun, "We're the life guard!"

When a vacuum roars like a dragon,
They laugh and curl, too strong to be bagged in.
"Is that your best? Come dance with me!"
A comedy show, just wait and see.

In every leaf, a giggle lies,
A tribute to joy, that never dies.
Growing wild, without a care,
Threads of laughter fill the air!

Portraits in Verdant Grace

Portraits painted, vibrant green,
Leaves like laughter, oh what a scene!
With every breeze, a sway, a bow,
"Look at us now!" they seem to vow.

Peering out from windows high,
They wink at clouds, as they drift by.
"Is that rain? Let's throw a ball!"
A party planned, they love it all.

In quirky poses, they stand so proud,
A leafy gallery, drawing a crowd.
Dancing shadows on the wall,
"Who's the fairest of them all?"

With roots so deep, yet spirits high,
They tell of joy as days go by.
In every green, a smile shown,
Portraits of love, in plant life grown!

Serenity in Sprawling Leaves

In a pot, proudly it leans,
Poking fun at my many flops.
Green arms stretching, like they're on scene,
Making dance floors of the tops.

A casual droop, a playful sway,
With each leaf, a giggle shared.
I chase my worries far away,
While its green vibes have me ensnared.

Dust bunnies scatter, my worries flee,
This leafy pal's got jokes to tell.
Who knew plants could make you feel free?
Well, this one surely does it well!

Sipping sun like a fancy drink,
I think it just winked at me!
A scene so silly, one might blink,
Nature's jesters, a sight to see!

The Indoor Sanctuary.

Nestled by windows, oh what a sight!
A dapper plant with charm galore.
Each green frond plays a game of light,
Still pretending it's out the door.

Pots of mischief, it seems to conspire,
With every inch, it stretches bold.
My home's jungle, did I inspire?
Or did it take charge—uncontrolled?

Caught in its web of leafy love,
I laugh as it reaches for the skies.
With every twist, a nudge from above,
It brings daily smiles and surprise.

As leaves spill over, a curtain drawn,
In this green sanctuary, I reign.
Who knew my decor would be so brawn?
An indoor haven, where joy is plain!

Whispers from the Green

Oh little plant with quirky flair,
You whisper secrets of the day.
Your leaves are gossip without a care,
In photosynthesis, you play!

With every curl, a story tells,
Of tango nights and breezy walks.
Dancing leaves, like magical spells,
It's got moves that tease and mock!

I swear you chuckle at my plight,
As I stumble with my watering can.
But there's no shame in your delight,
You know I'm your biggest fan!

From the corner, you reign supreme,
In this laughter-filled little den.
A whimsy plant, you are my dream,
Keeping me giggling once again!

Elegy of the Hanging Threads

With arms like octopi, no doubt,
This plant hangs low, a playful tease.
While I like to wander about,
It arches, like it owns the breeze.

Its strands cascade, a curtain drawn,
Calling me over, 'come and see!'
Who needs curtains when leaves have brawn?
This show-off plant's got victory!

As I stumble, get tangled too,
Its leafy tendrils gently sway.
They might just whisper, 'Hey, it's you!
Learn to dance like us today!'

So here we are, co-habitat,
With laughter woven tight in greens.
Oh plant of threads, so quirky, fat,
You're the laughter in my dreams!

www.ingramcontent.com/pod-product-compliance
Lightning Source LLC
Chambersburg PA
CBHW072129070526
44585CB00016B/1593